Reading for Today

A Sequential **4** Program for Adults

Program Authors	Jim Beers
	Linda Ward Beech
	Tara McCarthy
	Sam V. Dauzat
	Jo Ann Dauzat
Teacher's Edition Author	Norman Najimy
Program Consultant	Donna Amstutz
Program Advisors	Lonnie Farrell
	Aryola Taylor
	Adriana Figueroa
	Carol Paggi
	Jean Batey
	Ann Reed
	Sharon Darling
	Susan Paull

STECK-VAUGHN
COMPANY
A Subsidiary of National Education Corporation

Acknowledgements

The authors gratefully acknowledge Bob Greene, syndicated columnist for the *Chicago Tribune*. Our story on pages 84–85 and 93–95 is based on Bob's column entitled "Song of the Powder Room" in *American Beat*.

Photography:
Jim Myers—cover
Sandy Wilson—iv, 9, 11
Michael Patrick—14, 23, 25
Michael Murphy—28, 37, 39, 53
Cynthia Ellis—42
Bill Records—70, 75
Stan Kearl—86, 95
Cary Wolinsky/Stock, Boston—56
Owen Franken/Stock, Boston—67
Danuta Otfinowski/Jeroboam—64

ISBN: 0-8114-1908-8

Table of Contents

Do You Need To Buy It?

Pat: Say, Sis, what do we have to eat? I don't want to pay to eat out when I can eat at home.

Kay: Look up there and see. I get things all the time. I take a lot of time at the store finding good buys.

Pat: Well . . . I see eight cans of nuts, some hot dog buns, and a lot of pop. But these foods don't go together well. What is going on?

Kay: When I go to the store, I shop with these! They help me use my money well.

Pat: You are right. And these can help a lot when they are for things we need. But you are buying things that we don't need. You have to look at what we have. I don't like paying for something that we don't need.

Kay: I see—you want me to buy the things you want to eat, right? Maybe you need to do the shopping, Sis. That will help you see the problems I have to cope with!

Review Words

A. Check the words you know.

- ☐ 1. baseball
- ☐ 2. game
- ☐ 3. thing
- ☐ 4. because
- ☐ 5. many
- ☐ 6. need
- ☐ 7. buyer
- ☐ 8. sell
- ☐ 9. seven
- ☐ 10. these
- ☐ 11. see
- ☐ 12. want

B. Read and write these sentences.

1. Buyers like Kay want all the things they see.

_____

2. Do they buy because they need all these things?

_____

3. Kay does not need many of the things she buys.

_____

4. Did you see Kay buy seven tickets to the baseball game?

_____

_____

5. Store owners can make money when they sell to buyers like Kay.

_____

_____

C. Choose an answer from the words in the list.

1. a game played with a bat and ball _____

2. a person who buys _____

3. one more than six _____

4. something a child likes to play _____

Sight Words

could   save   coupon   then

▶ We <u>could</u> use <u>coupons</u> and <u>then</u> <u>save</u> money.

A. Read the sight words above and the example sentence. Underline the sight words in sentences 1–5 below.

1. I read the ads and then clip out the coupons.
2. Do I need to save all the coupons I see?
3. Could they help me save on something I need?
4. I could clip out the coupons I want to use.
5. Then I could use the coupons to get the things I need.

B. Choose the words below to finish the sentences.

save   then   coupons   could

1. You ———— give me some tips about using coupons.
2. Cutting out ———— can take a lot of time.
3. Save a lot of coupons and ———— go shopping.
4. You don't ———— money when you buy things that you don't need.

C. Practice reading the sentences. Underline the sight words.

Pat and Kay want to save money when they shop. One way they could save money is to use coupons. Pat finds coupons by reading the store ads, and then Kay clips out the ones that could help them save. They save a lot of coupons and then buy the things they need.

Sight Words

think	much	how	cost

▶ <u>How</u> <u>much</u> do you <u>think</u> meat will <u>cost</u>?

A. **Read the sight words above and the example sentence. Underline the sight words in 1—4 below.**

1. Many people could use coupons, but they don't think about it.
2. The right way to use coupons is to think about what you are buying.
3. How much money does meat cost without the coupon?
4. Will meat cost that much money at a different store?

B. **Choose the words below to finish the sentences.**

much	How	cost	think

1. _____ many coupons have you cut out?
2. I _____ the store will take our coupons.
3. How _____ meat do we need to buy?
4. Meat might _____ more at a different store.

C. **Read the sentences. Underline the sight words.**

Food costs more and more these days. I think we could save money by using coupons. But we have to think about some things when we shop. How much does food cost when we use coupons? Will the cost go down at a big store that has a lot of goods? How much trouble is it to get to that store?

Sight Words

roommate   why   spend   too

▶ <u>Why</u> does my <u>roommate</u> <u>spend</u> <u>too</u> much money?

A. Read the sight words above and the example sentence. Underline the sight words in 1−5 below.

1. My roommate saves all the coupons she sees.
2. Then she spends money for things we don't need.
3. When we shop together, she does not buy too much.
4. Why can't she do that when I'm not with her?
5. I think my roommate could learn to stop buying things we don't need.

B. Choose the words below to finish the sentences.

too   roommate   Why   spend

1. _____ do you think people save coupons?
2. Things cost _____ much money today.
3. I think that my _____ needs help shopping.
4. Why _____ more when you can save with coupons?

C. Read the sentences. Underline the sight words.

My roommate has a problem when she goes shopping without me. She spends money on things we don't need because she thinks she saves money. Then we have too many things, but not what we need. Why do store ads and coupons make people want things they can't use? I'm going to help my roommate quit buying things we don't need.

Phonics: Consonant Blends with *r*

A. **Listen to the beginning sound in each word below.**
Underline the letters that stand for the *r* blend.

br	cr	dr	fr
brand	cream	drive	friend
brag	crop	drug	from

gr	pr	tr	str
group	problem	trouble	street
gray	prison	truck	strut

B. **Make other words with *r* blends. Write each word**
and read it.

-ay   *-ip*

gr + ay = _____   dr + ip = _____

pr + ay = _____   gr + ip = _____

tr + ay = _____   str + ip = _____

str + ay = _____   tr + ip = _____

C. **Choose the right word for each sentence below.**

1. (bag, brag) Kay likes to _____ about the
   money she saves.

2. (trip, tip) Kay and I went on a big shopping

   _____ .

3. (brand, band) She used a coupon to buy a good

   _____ of hot dogs.

4. (ray, tray) We had a big _____ full of hot
   dogs to eat.

Phonics: -y and -ink

why

by

my

A. Read the words in the box. Make other -y words below.

cr + y = _____

dr + y = _____

fr + y = _____

tr + y = _____

B. Read the sentences. Write a -y word to finish each sentence.

1. I think _____ roommate uses too many coupons.

2. Kay said she will _____ not to buy food we don't need.

3. _____ did she buy all these hot dogs?

think

pink

rink

sink

A. Read the words in the box. Make other -ink words below.

w + ink = _____

br + ink = _____

dr + ink = _____

B. Read the sentences. Write an -ink word to finish each sentence.

1. When I was a child, I liked _____ pop.

2. My sister got 12 cans for us to _____.

3. I don't _____ we needed that much pop.

Irregular Verbs

save—saved   think—thought

We added -ed to some action words to show the past. Other words change the spelling to show the past. They are called irregular verbs.

Examples: I think of my sister. (I am doing it now).
            I thought of my sister a lot. (I did it in the past.)

A. Read these lists of action words (verbs).

Present	Past		Present	Past
sell	sold		are	were
make	made		find	found
give	gave		take	took
buy	bought		pay	paid
teach	taught		spend	spent

B. Practice reading the paragraph. Underline the irregular verbs.

   I gave some coupons to my roommate, and she took them to the store. Kay thought all the coupons were good, and she bought a lot of things. Then she found out the coupons were good in May, but not in June. I hope this taught Kay to read coupons well.

C. Complete each sentence by choosing the verb that tells about the past.

1. Someone at the store _____ my roommate a

   <u>sell   sold</u>

   new radio.

2. The trouble was that Kay _____ too much

   <u>pay   paid</u>

   for it.

The Cost of Saving

Kay: Pat, look at all these coupons! We could save big money this way. This is a good one . . . we buy seven cans of dog food and send in this coupon. Then they send us seven more cans!

Pat: That could be a good saving for us, Kay, but we don't <u>have</u> a dog!

Kay: OK . . . but this coupon is right for us. We can save ten cents on figs at the health food store. They cost much more at the store down the street.

Pat: Figs? Who likes figs in this home? What a roommate you are. You spend money on things

—Cost—

we don't need because you think you are getting a good buy. It ends up costing us money, not saving money!

Kay: OK, Pat, I see why you don't want me to buy things we don't need. Good buyers don't use all the coupons they see. But I may need help from you, Sis.

Pat: Then give me these ads! I'll find some coupons we can use. Say! We could win tickets to a baseball game in May with this coupon. All we need to do is cut out the coupons from the hot dogs we buy and send them in. What do you think?

Kay: You don't have to sell me on baseball. I love ball games . . . and hot dogs, too.

Pat: We'll have to buy many, many hot dogs, Kay, because we need 50 coupons to win the tickets.

[Many days go by . . .]

Kay: I don't think I like these hot dogs, Pat. Why don't we go out to eat?

Pat: We bought them to win the tickets for the baseball game. And we can't go out to eat because I spent all our food money on hot dogs.

Kay: But, Pat, how much can a person spend on hot dogs? And how many hot dogs can we eat without getting sick? Well, you do think we'll win, don't you?

Pat: We'll win something because we did what the coupon said. What more could we do?

—Cost—

[More days go by . . .]

Kay: Pat, look what came for us! It's from the coupon people, and I bet it's our tickets to the baseball game. I can tell this is our lucky day.

Pat: No! It can't be! Read this!

Kay: What is it, Pat? Is something wrong? Did we lose?

Pat: We did not lose, but we did not win the baseball tickets. We're getting more hot dogs! They are on the way to us.

Kay: I think I'm going to be sick. I'm sick of seeing hot dogs and coupons. This has taught me the right way to use coupons. I found out that trying to save money can sometimes cost me money. I have to think about what I'm buying.

Comprehension: Finding Facts

Tips for Finding Facts

Facts are things like names, dates, and numbers. What people think or feel about something is <u>not</u> a fact. To find facts in what you read, ask yourself:

- Who?
- What?
- How much/many?
- Where?
- When?

A. Find these facts in the story. Write the correct word on the line.

1. **Who** is Kay's roommate? _____

2. **What** do they want to win? _____

3. **How much** can they save on figs? _____

4. **Where** can they buy figs? _____

5. **When** is the baseball game? _____

B. Find these facts in the story. Write the correct word on the line.

1. Kay finds coupons in the _____.
   table   ads   home

2. Pat spent all her money on _____.
   dog food   pop   hot dogs

3. Pat wants to win _____.
   tickets   mugs   figs

4. Kay and Pat did win _____.
   money   hats   hot dogs

Life Skill: Reading Coupons

longer   ounces (oz.)   word

A. **Read the new words above. Then read the coupons below.**

1.

MANUFACTURER'S COUPON   NO EXPIRATION DATE

FAMILY SIZE NEW!

bright

171 OZ.

SAVE 50¢

WHEN YOU BUY
ONE FAMILY SIZE (171 oz.)
OR THREE REGULAR
SIZE (20 oz.)

50¢

0 16000 49980

2.

15¢

MANUFACTURER'S COUPON
Expires 8/8/87

SAVE 15¢

on a 16-oz. package of
Oscar-Buyer Hot Dogs

HOT DOGS OSCAR BUYER

HOT DOGS OSCAR BUYER

To the store owner:
Oscar Buyer Foods will give you
the value of this coupon and 7¢ for handling.
Customer will pay sales tax. This coupon is good
only on Oscar Buyer Hot Dogs.

15¢

B. **Read the questions and write the answers.**

1. One of the coupons is good for a longer time. Is it coupon 1 or coupon 2?

_____

2. What word does oz. stand for in both coupons?

_____

3. How much money can you save when you use

coupon 1? _____ coupon 2? _____

Who Needs To Read?

Mr. Sanders is a man who cannot read. He has learned to get by in life, but he feels that a person who can't read is disabled. Someday he wants to take the time to have someone teach him. Something he wants more than that is for his son, Jay, to learn to read well. He wants Jay's life to be different.

Jay has a problem with reading, too, but his family had not talked much about it. Then one night Jay told his dad that the teacher wanted to see his parents. It was time for the family to look into this problem.

When they sat at the table together that night, no one talked much. Jay looked down at his food without eating. Mrs. Sanders had a sad look. The time to talk had come, but no one said much. When a father can't read, how can he make his son learn?

Review Words

A. Check the words you know.

☐ 1. disabled ☐ 2. teach ☐ 3. gave
☐ 4. together ☐ 5. learn ☐ 6. said
☐ 7. someone ☐ 8. take ☐ 9. down
☐ 10. teacher ☐ 11. into ☐ 12. who

B. Read and write these sentences.

1. Will Jay be disabled because I can't teach him to read?

_____

2. I gave him help with baseball, but who will be his reading teacher?

_____

_____

3. When Jay takes time with his work, he does not get into trouble.

_____

_____

4. We'll all work together to help Jay learn to read.

_____

C. Match each word and its meaning.

_____ 1. down   a. a person

_____ 2. said   b. not up

_____ 3. someone   c. talked

Sight Words

school   always   must   mean

▶ Does this law <u>mean</u> that children <u>must</u> <u>always</u> go to <u>school</u>?

A. Read the sight words above and the example sentence. Underline the sight words in 1—5 below.

1. Mr. Sanders always wanted to go to school.

2. Going to school means you have a chance to learn.

3. Schools are not always for children.

4. A teacher must spend a lot of time helping people learn.

5. Does our teacher mean that we must always do well?

B. Choose the words below to finish the sentences.

must   always   mean   school

1. People don't have to go to _____ to learn.

2. Having a good teacher _____ helps you learn.

3. I _____ learn to read to help Jay.

4. Learning to read will _____ a chance for a good job.

C. Read the sentences. Underline the sight words.

Some parents think schools must always teach children to read. But children must get help at home with the things they learn at school. What does this mean for parents who can't read well? Sometimes these parents must go to school, too.

Sight Words

meet   soon   after   where

▶ Tell me <u>soon</u> <u>where</u> we can <u>meet</u> <u>after</u> school.

A. Read the sight words above and the example sentence. Underline the sight words in 1—5 below.

1. Mr. Sanders must meet his son's teacher soon.

2. Jay told his father where to find the teacher.

3. Mrs. Keating said she will meet Mr. Sanders.

4. Soon he will talk to her about Jay's problem.

5. After this talk, Mr. Sanders will see where he can help Jay.

B. Choose the words below to finish the sentences.

After   soon   Where   meet

1. _____ school is a good time for a parent to see a teacher.

2. Many teachers save this part of the day to _____ with parents.

3. Teachers don't go home _____ after the children.

4. _____ will Mr. Sanders find Jay's teacher?

C. Read the sentences. Underline the sight words.

Parents may have problems to work out when they meet with a teacher. They must find out where the school is and how to get there. Sometimes both the child and parents must find a time to meet together with the teacher. Parents might need to be at home soon after work. But, when parents and teachers find time for these meetings, they can work out ways to help a child.

Sight Words

or   report   grade   card

▶ Did Jay get a good <u>or</u> bad <u>grade</u> on his <u>report</u> <u>card</u>?

A. Read the sight words above and the example sentence. Underline the sight words in 1—5 below.

1. In school you may have to give a report.

2. Will you get a good or bad grade?

3. A report that makes the reader think will get a good grade.

4. Children don't get good grades on report cards because they are lucky.

5. Good grades on a report card mean the child did good work.

B. Choose the words below to finish the sentences.

card   or   report   grade

1. The teacher will like Jay's _____.

2. He won't get a bad _____ from the teacher.

3. Did Jay's parents see his report _____?

4. Were they glad _____ sad about his grades?

C. Read the sentences. Underline the sight words.

What does a good grade on a report card mean? Does it stand for luck or work? It means the child did a lot of work to get the grade. Some children have trouble giving a report. A parent can help by talking with the child about what to say in the report, or they can spend time reading it together. Soon the child will get good grades on report cards.

Phonics: Consonant Blends with s

A. **Listen to the beginning sound in each word below. Underline the letters that stand for the s blend.**

sc	sk	sl	sm
scat	skin	slip	smoke
scold	sky	sled	smell

sn	sp	st	sw
snip	spend	star	swim
snake	spell	store	sway

B. **Make other words with s blends. Write each word and read it.**

-ay   *-y*

sl + ay = _____   sk + y = _____

st + ay = _____   sl + y = _____

sw + ay = _____   sp + y = _____

C. **Choose the right word for each sentence below.**

1. (sell, spell) Jay must learn to _____ and read well.

2. (say, stay) He will _____ after school to get help from his teacher.

3. (star, tar) The teacher will give Jay a big gold _____ on his report.

4. (spend, send) Mr. Sanders wants to _____ time learning to read, too.

5. (cold, scold) Will Mr. Sanders _____ Jay about his grades?

Phonics: -eet and -ean

meet

beet

feet

street

A. Read the words in the box. Make other -eet words.

gr + eet = _____

sl + eet = _____

sw + eet = _____

B. Read the sentences. Write an -eet word to finish each sentence.

1. Mr. and Mrs. Sanders will go to Jay's school to

_____ his teacher.

2. His teacher is a _____ person who loves children.

3. She will _____ Mr. Sanders with a handshake.

mean

bean

clean

lean

A. Read the words in the box. Make other -ean words.

D + ean = _____

J + ean = _____

w + ean = _____

B. Read the sentences. Write an -ean word to finish each sentence.

1. Jay's teacher is Mrs. _____ Keating.

2. She isn't a _____ teacher, but she makes Jay do his own work.

3. When Jay learns to read, he won't have to

_____ on his friends for help.

Prefixes *re* - and *un* -

$$re + do = \text{redo} \qquad un + do = \text{undo}$$

A prefix is a word part added to the front of a word. The prefix gives the word a new meaning. The prefix *re* means to do again. The prefix *un* means not.

A. Add the prefix and write each new word.

Add *re*		**Add *un***	
read	_____	lucky	_____
mind	_____	sold	_____
pay	_____	fit	_____
run	_____	loved	_____

B. Practice reading the paragraph. Underline the words with prefixes.

Jay thinks he is unlucky to have a mean teacher. But someday he will want to repay her for her help. The teacher tells Jay that he must reread things many times. She makes him redo work that has mistakes in it.

C. Choose the correct word below to finish each sentence.

undo   remind   unfit   unloved

1. A person who can't read is _____ for many jobs.

2. I'll _____ my son to do his homework.

3. Jay will _____ all the teacher's work if he does not read at home.

4. When children get bad grades, they may feel

_____

The Report Card

They sat at the table together that night, but the Sanders family wasn't talking at all. Mr. Sanders did not look at his son Jay. Jay looked down at his food without eating.

"Well, Jay, it looks like we've got trouble," his father said in a sad way. "How could you get this grade on a report card? It says you can't read. The teacher gave you an *F* in reading and spelling."

"What can I say? I'm unlucky in school," Jay said. "Or maybe the teacher gave me a bad grade because she is mean." Then Jay looked up at his father. "Dad, why must I learn to read? After all, you can't read, and you always get by OK."

—Card—

Mr. Sanders could not say what he was feeling. All he could think about was how much he had always wanted to learn to read. When he was a child, he got a job and quit school. Then he was a family man. After that, he had no time for school.

"I can't tell you how much I want to read," he said. "A person who can't read is disabled. When I need to read something, I always have to get help from someone. You must learn to read, Jay."

"Well, my teacher wants to meet with you and Mother about the grades on my report card," Jay said.

A meeting with the teacher! That reminded Mr. Sanders of his own school days. He had had many problems in his life then. To this day, talking about teachers, grades, and school gave him trouble. But he wanted to help his son.

"I can go see her, but Mother needs to stay home with you," he said. "Where can I find the teacher?"

"She will be at the school tonight after seven," Jay said. "You can meet her in Room 10."

• • •

Mr. Sanders walked into Room 10 at a quarter after seven. A sweet-looking woman sat at the table. She looked up.

"I'm Mr. Sanders, Jay's father," he said. "I came about Jay's report card."

"Yes, Mr. Sanders. I was hoping you could come," the teacher greeted him. "I'm Jean Keating. Jay is having a lot of trouble in reading and spelling."

"Well, why don't you teach him to read?" Mr. Sanders said. "Isn't that a teacher's job?"

—Card—

"Yes, but I must teach many children. I can't let Jay take all my time. Jay needs a lot of help, and it can't all come from me. He needs help at home from you."

Mr. Sanders looked down. He did not want to tell her, but he must. "Mrs. Keating, I can't read. That is why I don't help Jay more. I always wanted to learn, but I don't know where to get help."

"There is a way you can help Jay. Let him teach you what he learns in school. Children learn a lot by getting to teach someone. But could you take having Jay for a teacher?" said Mrs. Keating.

"I think I could," Mr. Sanders said. "No, I can. We can learn to read together. Soon we will both be getting A's."

Mrs. Keating laughed with Mr. Sanders. "Well, you can always get an A from me in something—being a good father."

Comprehension: Main Idea

Tips for Finding the Main Idea

- Read the whole paragraph or story.
- Decide what the paragraph or story is about. The main idea is the point the writer is making. It tells the most important idea.
- Check the first part of the paragraph. Often, the first sentence is a clue to the main idea.

A. Pick the best choice for a new story title.

_____ Parents Are Teachers, Too

_____ Learning the Right Words

_____ Children and Homework

B. Underline the words that best complete each sentence.

1. Jay isn't learning to read well because
   a. he is unlucky.
   b. he thinks he can get by without reading, like his dad.
   c. his teacher is mean.

2. Jay's teacher can't spend more time with Jay because
   a. Jay has to work after school.
   b. she does not like him.
   c. she has many children to work with.

Life Skill: Reading Report Cards

best   worst   name   math

A. Read the new words above. Then read the report card below.

STUDENT'S NAME **Jay Sanders**   GRADE **3**

	Reporting Period					
	1	2	3	4	5	6
Reading	B	C	C⁻	F		
Comprehension	+	−	−	−		
Oral	+	−	−	−		
Does work on time	−	−	−	−		
Language	B	B	C	C		
Oral expression	+	+	−	−		
Written expression	+	+	−	−		
Does work on time	+	+	−	−		
Spelling	B	C	C⁻	F		
Mastery of spelling lists	+	−	−	−		
Does work on time	−	−	−	−		
Math	B	A	A⁻	A		

B. Read the questions and write the answers.

1. What did Jay make his best grade in?

   _____

2. What was Jay's worst grade? What was it in?

   _____

   _____

3. Does Jay do his work on time in reading and spelling? How do you know?

   _____

   _____

A Family Man

What a lucky day this is for me! It's more like a holiday than a workday. Today Maria told me that I'm going to be a father! When she told me, I gave her a big hug. We wanted to both laugh and cry.

I must tell my family and friends. My parents will want to buy lots of things for the child. I bet they'll try to spend too much money. After the child comes, Maria's parents will drive up from the city to help out. Her best friend from down the street will go with her to the clinic.

We must think of a name for our child. Maria wants to name the child after her mother. I want a son to be named after my best friend. It's good that we have some time to think about a name.

I have a lot to learn about being a father, but my own father taught me a lot about being a loving parent. Maria will need my help with the heavy work at home. I'll take her to see the doctor, and I'll buy the right foods for her to eat. She must be in good health when the child comes. We're both smokers, but we'll quit for the child's sake. I'll do what I can to give this child a good life. I have big hopes for this family.

Review Words

A. Check the words you know.

☐ 1. child ☐ 2. come ☐ 3. clinic
☐ 4. doctor ☐ 5. hope ☐ 6. smoker
☐ 7. drive ☐ 8. hug ☐ 9. parents
☐ 10. heavy ☐ 11. up ☐ 12. street

B. Read and write these sentences.

1. I gave Maria a hug when I learned about our child.

_____

_____

2. The doctor at the clinic said our child will come in June.

_____

_____

3. I'm a heavy smoker, but I hope to quit for our child's sake.

_____

_____

C. Choose a word from the list to complete the puzzle.

Down

1. not down
2. a trip in a car
3. a road

Across

4. mother and father

Sight Words

as	responsible	wife	baby

▶ As responsible parents, my wife and I will both look after our baby.

A. Read the sight words above and the example sentence. Underline the sight words in 1—5 below.

1. My wife Maria is doing what the doctor told her.
2. We're learning how to be responsible parents.
3. My wife stopped smoking because it isn't good for the baby.
4. As a mother-to-be, she must think of her health.
5. Responsible parents try to make a good life for children.

B. Choose the words below to finish the sentences.

wife	as	responsible	baby

1. My _____ and I will soon be parents.
2. Having a _____ means a lot to us.
3. We want to be _____ parents.
4. We'll try to spend _____ much time _____ we can with our child.

C. Read the sentences. Underline the sight words.

After my wife found out she was going to have a baby, we both stopped smoking. As soon as we learned what our smoking could do to the baby, we had to quit. We're responsible for our baby's health. As our child gets big, we'll feel responsible for the child's schooling as well.

Sight Words

before   new   know   small

▶ <u>Before</u> I'm a <u>new</u> father, I must <u>know</u> some things about <u>small</u> children.

A. Read the sight words above and the example sentence. Underline the sight words in 1—5 below.

1. Before you know it, we'll have a new baby.
2. Do you think the baby will know that I'm a new father?
3. To be a good father, I must learn many new things.
4. I need to know how to carry a small child.
5. What do new parents feed a small baby?

B. Choose the words below to finish the sentences.

Small   know   new   Before

1. _____ our baby comes, I need to learn how to be a good father.
2. Is there a school for _____ parents?
3. We need to _____ a lot of things.
4. _____ children need lots of help.

C. Practice reading the sentences. Underline the sight words.

We have a lot to think about before the baby comes. My wife and I will be responsible for a new life. Does a small child cry all night? Will I need to spend more time at home than I did before? We know our lives are going to be different, but we feel good about our new family.

Sight Words

pregnant   rock   tired   late

► Carrying a baby can make a <u>pregnant</u> woman feel <u>tired</u>.
We will <u>rock</u> our baby <u>late</u> into the night.

A. Read the sight words above and the example sentences. Underline the sight words in 1—4 below.

1. Maria's best friend Jan is pregnant, too.
2. Jan tells Maria that all pregnant women don't feel tired.
3. She says that the best thing to stop a crying baby is to rock it.
4. Jan says that new parents may feel tired from getting up late at night to feed the baby.

B. Choose the words below to finish the sentences.

tired   rock   late   pregnant

1. Get to the clinic before it's too _____!
2. Dad used to _____ me when I was small.
3. Can a new father get _____ of holding his baby?
4. A group of _____ women meets at the clinic.

C. Practice reading the sentences. Underline the sight words.

Maria was feeling tired, and she went to see the doctor about this. That was when she found out she is pregnant. I came home late that night, but she was up to tell me the good news. As soon as the baby comes, I want to spend time rocking our baby.

Phonics: Consonant Blends with *l*

A. Listen to the beginning sound in each word below. Underline the letters that stand for the *l* blend.

bl	cl	fl
blend	clinic	fly
blink	clan	flag

gl	pl	sl
glad	player	sly
gland	plan	sleet

B. Make other words with *l* blends. Write each word and read it.

-ink   *-ight*

bl + ink = _____   bl + ight = _____

cl + ink = _____   fl + ight = _____

pl + ink = _____   pl + ight = _____

sl + ink = _____   sl + ight = _____

C. Choose the right word for each sentence below.

1. (pan, plan) We need to _____ a name for the baby.

2. (plight, light) Staying up all night to rock the baby is the _____ of new parents.

3. (lad, glad) We're _____ that we'll have the chance to be good parents.

Phonics: -ock and -ate

---

rock

lock

mock

sock

A. Read the words in the box. Make other -ock words below.

bl + ock = _____

cl + ock = _____

sm + ock = _____

B. Read the sentences. Write an -ock word to finish each sentence.

1. Carlos plans to _____ the baby at night.

2. Maria got a big _____ to fit her.

3. Carlos looks at the _____. Is it time to go to the clinic?

4. Our baby will play with the _____ we made.

---

late

date

gate

rate

A. Read the words in the box. Make other -ate words below.

pl + ate = _____

sk + ate = _____

st + ate = _____

B. Read the sentences. Write an -ate word to finish each sentence.

1. I hope that our baby won't wake up _____ at night.

2. We have a _____ to see the doctor today.

3. The baby won't eat from a _____ for a long time.

Plurals with -*ies*

baby + **ies** = babies   **city** + **ies** = cities

We add *s* to some words to mean more than one. If a word ends in a consonant plus *y*, we usually change the *y* to *i* and add *es* to mean more than one.

A. Read the words and write the word that means more than one.

One	More Than One	
1. baby	babies	_____
2. family	families	_____
3. cry	cries	_____
4. city	cities	_____
5. try	tries	_____
6. country	countries	_____

B. Practice reading the paragraph. Underline the words that end in -*ies*.

Maria's parents and mine were from different countries. Then they came to this country, but they were in different cities. Our families did not meet before our wedding.

C. Choose the plural word that completes each sentence.

cries   babies   countries   families

1. Our _____ will be glad about the baby.

2. We won't mind when the baby's _____ wake us.

3. Someday we want to have more _____.

4. Many _____ have laws that help children.

The Time Has Come

Maria: Carlos, before the end of the day, we'll be new parents. I can't help thinking about the day we found out I was pregnant.

Carlos: We were both glad, and our families were, too. How are you feeling? Do you want me to call the clinic and tell the doctor we'll be right there?

Maria: No, it's not time yet. You know, Carlos, we have not thought of a name for the baby. We'll need to have a name soon.

Carlos: I know . . . but I can't think of the right one. All I can think of is you. I hope that you don't have problems when the baby comes.

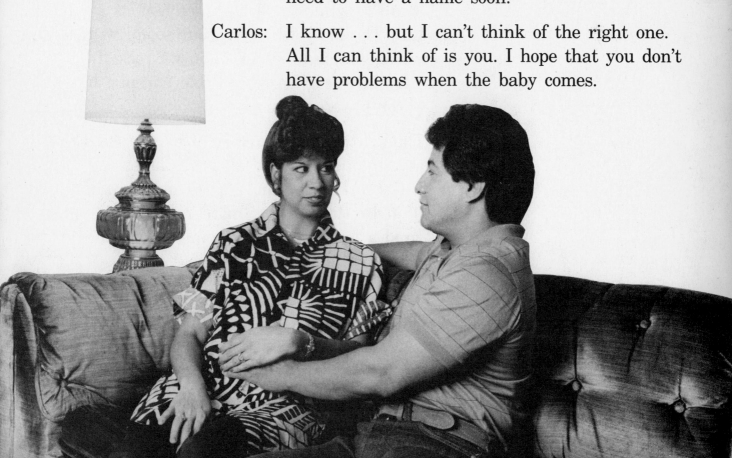

—Time—

Maria: The doctor says the baby and I are both fine. I did as I was told at the clinic. I walked up and down our street two times a day. I did not carry heavy things or get too tired. And I did not drive the car on big trips. The chances are good that I'll have no trouble when the baby comes.

Carlos: The doctor says it's a good thing that we stopped smoking when we learned that you are pregnant. When parents are smokers, small children in the home can get sick. As responsible parents, we had to quit.

Maria, I have big plans for this child. I've stocked our home with baby food and lots of small playthings. My brother lent us a baby bed. The baby will be in our room, with a rocker for us to sit in when we rock the baby. I hope we can be responsible parents, like our parents were for us.

Maria: I know that we can be, Carlos, but having a small child won't be all fun. Babies cry at all times of the day and night, and they have to be fed on time. New mothers and fathers feel tired a lot. Yes, this is going to be a new way of life for us.

Carlos: I'm lucky to have a wife who knows a lot about having a family. When you were a child, you had small brothers and sisters at home. That will help us both.

–Time–

Maria: You know, there will be many times when our baby will need our help. We'll have to teach our child right from wrong. Children need help from parents to do well in school. And they need lots of hugs!

Maria: It's a lot of work to be a responsible parent, but it will be fun, too.

Carlos: Right. It will feel good to see our child learn to walk and talk. When our baby wakes up late at night, I'll be there to help you rock the baby. I hope this child gets here soon!

Maria: Carlos . . . I think you are going to get what you want. You must drive me to the clinic . . .

Carlos: Doctor! My wife is about to have the baby. We'll meet you at the clinic. Don't be late!

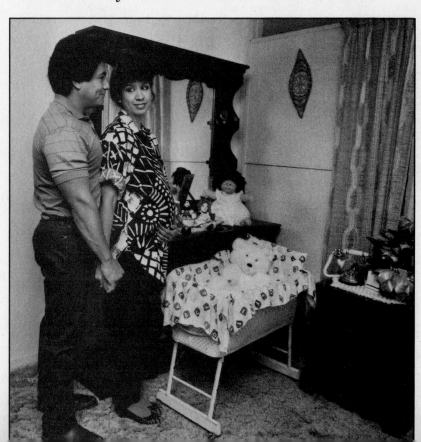

Comprehension: Main Idea

Tips for Finding the Main Idea

- Read the whole paragraph or story.
- Decide what the paragraph or story is about. The main idea is the point the writer is making. It tells the most important idea.
- Check the first part of the paragraph. Often, the first sentence is a clue to the main idea.

A. Pick the best choice for a new story title.

———— Responsible Parents

———— Clinic Work

———— Playing With Baby

B. Underline the words that best complete each sentence.

1. Carlos and Maria
   a. do not want to have children.
   b. want to be responsible, loving parents.
   c. think having a baby will be all fun.

2. Carlos thinks that his parents
   a. were loving, responsible parents.
   b. did not love him.
   c. will not be happy about the baby.

3. When the baby wakes up at night,
   a. Maria will be the one to rock the baby.
   b. Maria and Carlos will let the baby cry.
   c. Maria and Carlos will both help with the baby.

Life Skill: Reading Prescriptions

tablets   should   daily

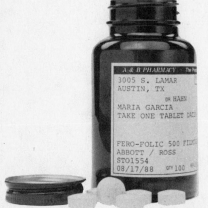

A. **Read the new words above. Then read the label below.**

A & B PHARMACY   The Prescription Center

3005 S. LAMAR	PH. 443-7534
AUSTIN, TX	

DR. HAHN

MARIA GARCIA
TAKE ONE TABLET DAILY.

FERO-FOLIC 500 FILMTABS
ABBOTT / ROSS
STO1554
08/17/88   QTY 100   REFILLS CALL

CAUTION: FEDERAL LAW PROHIBITS THE TRANSFER OF THIS DRUG TO ANY PERSON OTHER THAN THE PATIENT FOR WHOM IT WAS PRESCRIBED

B. **Read the questions and write the answers.**

1. How many of these tablets should Maria take daily?

   _____

2. What should Maria do to get more of these tablets?

   _____

   _____

3. What does *qty.* stand for? What does it mean?

   _____

   _____

4. The doctor gave Maria these tablets because she was feeling tired. Maria's father has been feeling tired, too. Should he take some of Maria's tablets? Why or why not?

   _____

   _____

   _____

Who Are They?

The people of our land are all different, and that is one of the best things about a big country. We could learn a lot from being together. Then why do we always want to be with people who are like we are? We see someone with different skin and we may not want to be friends. Disabled people may feel that they are not a part of the group. People from the country may think they don't like people from the city. It might not be right, but sometimes we don't feel at home with people who are different from us.

Should things be this way? Our country has room for many different groups. We may think they are different, but our daily lives are alike in many ways.

The men and women in the Baker family are from a small city. The families there all do things together, and they are not used to seeing new people. Maybe that is why things got out of hand that hot day in June. Two families were having an outing by the lake. By sundown, there was a big problem.

Review Words

A. Check the words you know.

- □ 1. bag
- □ 2. part
- □ 3. player
- □ 4. were
- □ 5. hip
- □ 6. camera
- □ 7. truck
- □ 8. day
- □ 9. sundown
- □ 10. tapes
- □ 11. June
- □ 12. different

B. Read and write these sentences.

1. In June, my wife and I were part of a big family outing.

   _____

   _____

2. We took two big bags of food, a tape player with tapes, and our camera.

   _____

   _____

3. When my wife got out of the truck, she slipped and landed on her hip.

   _____

   _____

C. Match the word and its opposite.

_____ 1. day		a. sunup
_____ 2. sundown		b. alike
_____ 3. different		c. night
_____ 4. part		d. all

Sight Words

summer   foreign   saw   around

▶ This <u>summer</u> we <u>saw</u> many <u>foreign</u> people <u>around</u> the city.

A. **Read the sight words above and the example sentence. Underline the sight words in 1—3 below.**

1. Some friends of mine went to a foreign country this summer.
2. They did not know how to get around and had trouble talking to the foreign people.
3. As soon as they could get around without much help, my friends saw a lot of the city.

B. **Choose the words below to finish the sentences.**

saw   Summer   foreign   around

1. _____ is a good time to take a trip.
2. How do you feel about people who come from a _____ country?
3. On our trip we _____ a lot of foreign people.
4. Some people like to take trips where they can go _____ together in a small group.

C. **Read the sentences. Underline the sight words.**

My family has been in this country for some time. But when they came here, it was a foreign land to them. They saw many new things. They did not know how to get around in a big city. They were not used to the hot summers. They were foreigners, but they saw this foreign land as a chance for a new life.

Sight Words

thank   snack   cook   picnic

▶ We must <u>thank</u> the <u>cook</u> who made the <u>snacks</u> for our <u>picnic</u>.

A. Read the sight words above and the example sentence. Underline the sight words in 1—4 below.

1. We found a good cook for the picnic.
2. After we meet the cook, we should thank him for the snacks.
3. When I go to a picnic, I don't mind the bugs.
4. After all, what is a picnic without a big bug or two?

B. Choose the words below to finish the sentences.

snacks   cook   thank   picnic

1. This summer we had a big family _____.
2. It's a lot of work to _____ the food for a family group.
3. I should _____ my brothers and sisters for helping me.
4. The _____ were the best part of the picnic.

C. Practice reading the sentences. Underline the sight words.

This summer we saw some foreigners having a family picnic. They don't cook like we do, but the food looked good. They saw us walking around and said we could have some of the picnic snacks. These foreign people made us feel like a part of the family. We thanked them before we went on our way.

Sight Words

jump   grass   rules   park

▶ The <u>park</u> <u>rules</u> say we can't walk on the <u>grass</u>. The children run down to the dock and <u>jump</u> in the water.

A. Read the sight words above and the example sentences. Underline the sight words in 1—4 below.

1. I got a summer job working in the city park.

2. I spend a lot of time cutting the grass.

3. Sometimes I want to jump in the lake and swim.

4. The park has rules that all people should read.

B. Choose the words below to finish the sentences.

park   rules   grass   jump

1. On a summer day, many people go to the

   _____ .

2. They _____ in the lake when they get too hot.

3. Will they let us sit on the _____ in this park?

4. We should read the _____ to find out.

C. Practice reading the sentences. Underline the sight words.

People use the park in different ways. Sometimes they sit on the grass or swim in the lake. Children like to run around on the dock and jump in the cold water. The park is owned by the city, and we have set up some rules. Because we all want to have a good time, we do as the rules say.

Phonics: Consonant Digraphs

A. Listen to the beginning sound in each word below. Underline the letters that stand for the beginning sound.

ch	sh	shr
chance	shy	shrug
child	shake	shrink

th	th	wh
then	thank	when
that	thing	why

B. Make other words with _ch_, _sh_, _shr_, _th_, and _wh_. Write each word and read it.

_-in_

ch + in = _____

sh + in = _____

th + in = _____

-ine

sh + ine = _____

shr + ine = _____

wh + ine = _____

C. Choose the right word for each sentence below.

1. (shine, shrine) I hoped for the sun to _____ the day we went to the park.

2. (hat, that) We were lucky _____ the sun came out, and we had a good day.

3. (sin, shin) We saw a small child fall down and hit her _____ on the rocks.

4. (whine, wine) She was a good child; she did not _____ .

Phonics: -*ack* and -*ank*

---

snack

back

pack

sack

A. Read the words in the box. Make other -*ack* words below.

bl + ack = _____

sh + ack = _____

wh + ack = _____

B. Read the sentences. Write an -*ack* word to finish each sentence.

1. The Baker family will _____ a picnic bag.

2. They carry the food to the park in a big

   _____.

3. They like to go _____ to the old tables by the lake.

---

thank

bank

sank

A. Read the words in the box. Make other -*ank* words below.

bl + ank = _____

dr + ank = _____

sp + ank = _____

B. Read the sentences. Write an -*ank* word to finish each sentence.

1. Mrs. Baker likes to sit by the _____ of the lake.

2. The children _____ cold water when they got hot.

3. Mr. Baker did not _____ his son for running down to the dock.

Suffixes -*ful* and -*ness*

help + ful = helpful   **good + ness = goodness**

A suffix is a word part added to the end of a word that changes the meaning of the word. *Ful* usually means filled with. Adding -*ness* to a word changes the word from a describing word to a naming word.

A.   Add the suffix and write each new word.

Add -*ness*		**Add -*ful***	
1. bold	_____	1. hand	_____
2. neat	_____	2. car	_____
3. sad	_____	3. hope	_____
4. sick	_____	4. play	_____
5. shy	_____	5. use	_____

B.   Practice reading the paragraph. Underline the words with -*ful* and -*ness*.

I'm hopeful that we'll have a good day for our picnic. I'm glad there is no sickness in the family. I've told the children to be helpful with the food when we get to the park. Children should have fun, but they know they must be useful, too.

C.   Choose the correct word below to finish each sentence.

carful   playful   handful   goodness

1. We have a _____ of people to take to the park.

2. Thank _____ Dad has a big van.

3. Much of the time my children are good, but

   sometimes they are a _____ .

Helpful Foreigners

It was a good day to have a picnic in the park. This part of the country was hot in June, and the Bakers were glad to be by the lake. Before a big family outing like this, Kate Baker always did a lot of shopping. She bought bags and bags of food, with lots of snacks for the children. Because they all liked music, she had someone in the family take a tape player. As she always did, she reminded Jack to get the camera.

When they got to the park, Kate reminded Reed and Nell about the park rules. Jack Baker told his children to mind the lifeguard at all times and to come right back to the picnic tables after swimming. Then Kate and Jack let the children run down to the dock and jump in the water. They did not want the children to get out of sight.

The Bakers were always lucky about getting the picnic tables by the lake. They liked these tables because no one was around. But this summer there were three new tables by the lake. When the Bakers got to the park, a new family was sitting at the tables. These people were different. From the way they talked, the Bakers could tell they were foreigners.

"I don't like it," Jack said. "Look at them. Look at the way that woman holds her baby on her hip. They are not from this country."

—Foreigners—

Jack was mad about the foreign family, but he did not know why. They had three playful children who were running around and yelling. The food they were cooking smelled different, and they had a big, old truck that looked like it was falling apart.

The trouble came at sundown when Jack called the children back from the lake. Jack saw that his son Reed was running and yelling in fright. The foreign man had run after Reed and was holding him down on the grass.

"What are you doing to my son?" Jack yelled. Was the foreign man trying to get his son? Then Reed sat up on the grass with tape on his hand.

"I fell and cut my hand. This man helped me," Reed said.

"This child cut his hand on the top of an old can," said the foreign man. "It will mend soon. I'm a doctor at the clinic in the city, and I treat many children. He will be OK."

"We can help our own children," Jack said. "What gives you the right to treat my child?"

The helpful foreign man looked at Jack without talking. Then he said, "Maybe I don't have the right to treat this child but, as a doctor, I'm responsible for doing something to help. You have been looking at us all day," he went on. "I know we look different from you, but we like the park, like you do. We like picnics, like you do. And we love children and want to help when they are in trouble."

—Foreigners—

Jack looked down. "I was wrong. I should thank you for helping Reed. Thank goodness you are a doctor! Will you shake my hand?"

"Yes," the man said, and they both laughed. After that, Mrs. Baker took some food to the new family. The children skipped around the tables. The parents could see that the children got used to playing together in no time at all.

Comprehension: Sequence

Tips on Sequence

Sequence is about time. It means the 1-2-3 order in which things happen. Use these hints to find the sequence of events in a story:

- Look for time words like *before, when, after, then, always, soon.*
- Look for words that end in *-ed.* They tell what happened before (in the past).
  Example: The children jump*ed* in the water.

A. **Write 1, 2, and 3 to show the order in which things happened in the story.**

_____ Reed fell and cut his hand.

_____ The Bakers saw a new family sitting at the picnic tables.

_____ Kate Baker bought lots of snacks.

B. **Underline the words that best complete each sentence.**

1. The Baker children learned the park rules
   a. after Reed fell down.
   b. before Kate and Jack let them run to the dock.
   c. when they went shopping with Mrs. Baker.
2. Mrs. Baker took some food to the new family
   a. before sundown.
   b. when she saw the new family at the tables.
   c. after the doctor helped Reed.

Life Skill: Reading Park Rules

first   **most**   **other**

A. **Read the new words above. Then read the rules below.**

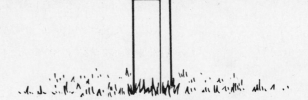

PARK RULES

1. No picnics on the grass; use the tables by the lake. Clean up picnic tables after you eat.

2. No running on the dock. Children must mind the lifeguard at all times.

3. No eating or drinking by the water.

4. No yelling or fighting.

5. Don't walk, sit, or smoke on the grass.

6. All cars must be out of the park by 10 P.M.

B. **Read the questions and write the answers.**

1. Do you think most parks have rules like these? Why?

   _____

   _____

2. What is the first thing parents should do when they take the family to the park?

   _____

   _____

3. What rules have to do with eating or drinking?

   _____

   _____

4. What other rules might you see in a park?

   _____

Like It Is

I'm thinking about Chet and Hank and the friends they have. These kids want to be big men, but they are spending time with people who can get them in trouble. They remind me of my life at that age. First, I was arrested for shoplifting. Soon I got into more trouble. Then I ended up in a prison uniform.

I talked to my friend Sly after the meeting. Chet and Hank both came, but we could not tell how much they got out of it. They came because a social worker said they must. They are skipping school, and some of Chet's friends use drugs. Some store owners around the school think Chet and Hank are shoplifting music tapes.

We told them about prison—about the guards, the uniforms, and the cells. We wanted to make them see that prison life isn't like the movies. Most of the time, you have nothing to do. The lucky prisoners work in the prison shop. Most of the others sit around all day in this prison.

Is there hope for Hank and others like him? Who knows? Without someone to tell them how things are, they'll be seeing us again—for a longer stay.

Review Words

A. Check the words you know.

- ☐ 1. came
- ☐ 2. guard
- ☐ 3. uniform
- ☐ 4. men
- ☐ 5. prison
- ☐ 6. shoplift
- ☐ 7. more
- ☐ 8. there
- ☐ 9. social worker
- ☐ 10. life
- ☐ 11. movie
- ☐ 12. without

B. Read and write these sentences.

1. Some social workers came to see Sly and me.

_____

_____

2. They want to make a movie about life in prison.

_____

_____

3. Without our help, more people will end up in prison uniforms.

_____

_____

C. Choose an answer from the words in the list.

1. not here, but . . .   _____

2. take something without paying for it   _____

3. people who are not women   _____

4. a person who works in a prison   _____

Sight Words

here	kids	been	straight

▶ I've <u>been</u> <u>straight</u> with the <u>kids</u> who come <u>here</u>.

A. Read the sight words above and the example sentence. Underline the sight words in sentences 1–5 below.

1. I want these kids to go straight.
2. I've been telling them what my life here is like.
3. I feel like I've been in this prison uniform all my life.
4. Sly tells the kids that he has been in and out many times.
5. This time the law says he is here for good.

B. Choose the words below to finish the sentences.

straight	been	here	kid

1. Sly has _____ in prison much of his life.
2. He was locked up for shoplifting when he was a

   _____.

3. I hope I can go _____ when I get out.
4. Life _____ is no picnic.

C. Practice reading the sentences. Underline the sight words.

They send problem kids here, and our job is to set the kids straight. I do this because no one helped me when I was a kid. I like to think that my life here has been useful to someone. I think I've been responsible for helping some kids.

Sight Words

sentence	long	put	away

▶ They gave me a <u>long</u> <u>sentence</u> and <u>put</u> me
<u>away</u>.

A. **Read the sight words above and the example sentence. Underline the sight words in 1—4 below.**

1. One mistake can put a kid away for a long time.

2. When kids get arrested, they may think they are lucky to get a light sentence.

3. Let me tell you, a light sentence is a long time.

4. My sentence will keep me here a long time.

B. **Choose the words below to finish the sentences.**

sentence	away	put	long

1. When a man is _____ away, it stays on his record for life.

2. He finds out that a prison _____ is a ticket to nowhere.

3. It's a _____ time for him to spend with no life of his own.

4. I hope the kids in this group will go _____ and not end up in prison.

C. **Read the sentences. Underline the sight words.**

Sly was put away for life. That is a long time. My sentence will be up soon, and I hope I can make it OK out there. When you are away from family and friends, you lose track of them. It may take me a long time to find a job.

Sight Words

pick	still	again	lesson

▶ The guards know that many kids <u>still</u> don't learn our <u>lesson</u>. They can <u>pick</u> out the kids we're going to see <u>again</u>.

A. Read the sight words above and the example sentences. Underline the sight words in 1–5 below.

1. We try to teach these kids a lesson about prison.
2. Some of them still think that doing time makes you a big man.
3. We tell them to think again about prison.
4. There is still time for kids to learn that lesson.
5. They might pick up on what we're saying.

B. Choose the words below to finish the sentences.

still	pick	again	lesson

1. Sly and I learned our _____ late in life.

2. Our talk makes these kids sit _____ and think about life in prison.

3. We shake them up _____ and _____.

4. I can't always _____ out the ones who will go straight.

C. Read the sentences. Underline the sight words.

Some kids still think they can beat the law. We try to teach them a lesson before they get picked up by the cops. Sometimes I get tired of trying because they make mistakes again and again. Going straight and being responsible is still foreign to these kids.

Phonics: Syllables

A. **Read the words. Listen to the parts in each word. Some words have one part (syllable); some have two parts (syllables).**

One Syllable	Two Syllables	
save	coupon	cou-pon
spend	roommate	room-mate
must	after	af-ter
grade	report	re-port
health	sentence	sen-tence

B. **Read each word. Listen to the word parts (syllables). Then write the word under the correct heading.**

always
before
pregnant
school
lesson
wife
black
straight
picnic
guard

One Syllable

1. _____
2. _____
3. _____
4. _____
5. _____

Two Syllables

1. _____
2. _____
3. _____
4. _____
5. _____

C. **Read the sentences. Draw one line under one-syllable words. Draw two lines under two-syllable words.**

1. In prison, life is no picnic.

2. They lock you away from other people.

3. You get homesick, and you want to be with friends.

4. Sometimes you give up hope of getting out.

5. I plan to go straight when I get out of prison.

Phonics: -ick and -ill

pick

kick

lick

quick

sick

A. Read the words in the box. Make other -ick words.

sl + ick = _____

st + ick = _____

th + ick = _____

B. Write an -ick word to finish each sentence.

1. That guard likes to _____ on me.

2. No one will _____ up for me.

3. Prison life makes me _____ .

4. There is no _____ way out of a prison sentence.

still

bill

fill

kill

will

A. Read the words in the box. Make other -ill words.

ch + ill = _____

gr + ill = _____

sk + ill = _____

sp + ill = _____

B. Write an -ill word to finish each sentence.

1. Doing time in prison can _____ you.

2. You must find some way to _____ up the time.

3. I get a cold _____ when I think of the kids in here.

4. But some _____ don't learn the lesson.

Suffixes -*ly* and -*y*

friend + ly = friendly   **health + y = healthy**

Ly and -*y* are suffixes. *Ly* words usually tell how something is done. *Y* means full of or like. These suffixes are added to words to describe people or things.

A. Add the suffix and write each new word.

Add -*ly*		Add -*y*	
different	_____	grass	_____
bad	_____	boss	_____
cost	_____	hand	_____
father	_____	jump	_____
like	_____	rock	_____

B. Practice reading the sentences. Underline the words that end in -*y* or -*ly*.

I talked to Chet in a fatherly way because he was jumpy. I wanted him to see things differently. Some of Chet's friends are likely to get him in trouble. I did not want to be bossy, but I told him not to make the costly mistakes that I had made.

C. Choose the correct words to complete the sentences.

bossy   handy   friendly

1. Some people think that shoplifting is a

_____ way to get what you want.

2. These people may look _____ to Chet, but they'll get him in trouble.

3. I feel _____ when I make these kids learn our lesson.

Hank's Lesson

Well, a new group of kids came to meet with us today, and there was Hank again.

"What are you doing back here, man?" I grilled him. "Are you still in trouble with the law? How many more lessons do you need?"

I could see that the kid was jumpy. Sly and I did our part, telling the other kids about life in prison. Hank sat away from the group. Our lesson wasn't sinking in for him.

My mind went back to my own life at Hank's age. I was mad about a lot of things, and I wanted to fight back at life. I did not want to play by other people's rules. My first mistake was shoplifting, but my worst mistake was selling drugs. The law puts you away for a long time for that one.

—Lesson—

After we talked to the group, I stayed to meet with Hank and his social worker. I found out what was going on in Hank's life. After he'd been here the first time, he got into drugs and was arrested again. They could have handed the kid a heavy sentence, but he was lucky. His social worker gave Hank a chance to work things out, as long as he came to our prison talk again. He still needed to get the lesson straight.

"Straight life is no fun," said Hank. "Where does it get me? I hate school, and the teachers always pick on me. I can't read, and I've been faking it for a long time with my lessons. The men in my family don't help. My father and brothers are always on my back. Again and again they yell at me about my grades. When I take my report card home, I know I'm going to get a licking. My friends and I are sick of school and home. We get our kicks where we can, man!"

I thought about Hank's words. The kid was thinking of nothing but "kicks." He wanted a quick way out of his problems. A chill went up my spine. Thinking that way can get you into more trouble than you can cope with. I know—I've been there.

Hank and Sly and I had a long talk. This time I put things differently.

"You are right, kid," I said, "life isn't like the movies. You can make a lot of costly mistakes, but there are two ways to go, and *you* are responsible for *you*. You can learn to cope with life's problems, or you can end up in here."

"I'll think about it," Hank said as he shrugged.

—Lesson—

Sly looked at him coldly. "Who are you kidding? How many chances do you think you are going to get, kid? You may *think* you know about bad times, but when you've been here as long as I have . . . well, you will see. Daily life is a drag. Guards with guns are always around. You get tired of prison uniforms and prison food. You can't get away from people; still you are lonely. Some of the men in here could kill you without thinking about it first. You still have a chance, kid. Pick a different way of life."

As Hank walked away, Sly and I sat without talking. Will the kid go straight, or will he go for a prison sentence? I hope Hank will learn the lesson before it's too late.

Comprehension: Sequence

> ## Tips on Sequence
>
> Sequence is about time. It means the 1-2-3 order in which things happen. Use these hints to find the sequence of events in a story:
>
> - Look for time words like *before, when, after, then, always, again, soon, still.*
> - Look for words that end in *-ed*. They tell what happened before (in the past).
> - Look for action words used with *will*. They tell what may happen soon (in the future).

A. **Write 1, 2, and 3 to show the order in which things happened in the story.**

_____ Sly talked straight to Hank.

_____ Hank came back to the prison with a new group.

_____ Hank used drugs and was arrested again.

B. **Underline the words that complete each sentence.**

1. Hank came back to the prison group
   a. when Sly was talking.
   b. after he got arrested for drug use.
   c. before he got in trouble with the law.

2. The prisoners had a meeting with Hank
   a. before they talked to the group.
   b. when the social worker went home.
   c. after they quit talking to the new group.

Life Skill: Using a Phone Book

heading   toll   which

A. Read the new words above. Then read the list of phone numbers below.

HELPFUL NUMBERS

COUNSELING & GUIDANCE SERVICES

Austin Child Guidance & Evaluation Center	476-6015
Austin Rape Crisis Center	472-7273
Big Brothers & Sisters Inc.	451-6215
Child Assault Prevention Project	472-4651
Counseling & Pastoral Care	451-7337
Crisis Intervention Center & Information Hotline	472-4357
MHMR-Austin Travis County Outpatient Services	
North	452-9571
Central	476-7263
East	474-2481
South	447-2055
Service Corps Of Retired Executives (SCORE-ACE)	482-5111
Suicide Prevention Center	472-4357
Williamson County Crisis Center	255-1212
Womenspace	472-3053
Youth Advocacy Program	385-3325

FAMILY & CHILD SERVICES

AFDC Food Stamps Social Services	
North Office	929-7350
South Office	444-0511
Child & Family Service Inc.	478-1648
Extend-A-Care Inc	454-3651
Infant-Parent Training Program	472-3142
Junior Helping Hand Home For Children	459-3353
LaLeche League	836-9060
Marywood Maternity & Adoption Services	472-9251
Mother's Milk Drive Inc.	451-5560
Parents Without Partners Inc	459-5573
Travis County Children's Protective Services	834-0034
Women Infants And Children-WIC-Austin Travis County Health Department	474-1526
Workers Against Child Abuse Hot Line Toll Free-Dial 1 & Then	800-252-5400

B. Read the questions and write the answers.

1. Which heading is mostly about helping children?

_____

2. You think a parent is badly beating a child. Where could you call for help?

_____

3. Look at the last line on the right. What does "Toll Free" mean? What does "Hot Line" mean?

_____

_____

_____

Lonely in a Group

I walk from room to room. Sometimes I carry a drink to have something to do with my hands. People walk by me and say, "How are you?" I say, "Fine," but I don't mean it. They might think I'm having a good time, but I'm faking it. I feel shy and lonely.

I don't know one person here but my wife. Unlike me, she knows many people, and they all like her. I can see her laughing and chatting with her boss and some of her friends. I think they are talking about things at work.

I have trouble trying to talk with people I don't know. I feel differently with my own friends. I feel at home with them because I know they like me.

My wife says that learning to be a good talker is a skill. She tells me not to give up on this problem, but does she know what it's like to be shy? It's like walking down a long road with no end in sight. But in time, maybe I'll find a way to get over this problem.

Review Words

A. Check the words you know.

- [ ] 1. road
- [ ] 2. sometimes
- [ ] 3. fine
- [ ] 4. give
- [ ] 5. lonely
- [ ] 6. own
- [ ] 7. wife
- [ ] 8. problem
- [ ] 9. carry
- [ ] 10. does
- [ ] 11. talker
- [ ] 12. person

B. Read and write these sentences.

1. Sometimes I have problems talking to a person I don't know.

_____

_____

2. My own wife tells me I can be a fine talker, but it does not help me.

_____

_____

3. Being in a big group gives me a lonely feeling.

_____

_____

C. Choose words from the list to complete the puzzle.

Across

1. take from one spot to another
3. one who talks

Down

2. a street

Sight Words

ask   better   over   would

▶ I'll <u>ask</u> my friend Fran to help me get <u>over</u> this problem. Then I <u>would</u> feel <u>better</u> about being in big groups.

A. Read the sight words above and the example sentences. Underline the sight words in 1—5 below.

1. My wife is a lot better talker than I am.

2. I would like to be a better talker.

3. Who can I ask to help me get over this problem?

4. I can ask my friend Fran to help me.

5. I could not ask for a better friend than Fran.

B. Choose the words below to finish the sentences.

ask   would   over   better

1. I _____ like to have a good time in a group of new people.

2. I can _____ Fran to help me learn how to make new friends.

3. I'll get _____ tips from her.

4. Fran can help me get _____ feeling lonely in a big group.

C. Read the sentences. Underline the sight words.

Would you feel lonely in a big group of people? I would. Fran says I'd better learn to talk. Over and over again she tells me this, "Walk around, and soon you'll meet a person who would like to chat." I'm glad I asked Fran to give me some tips.

Sight Words

party   every   bring   never

▶ My wife <u>brings</u> me to <u>every</u> <u>party</u>, but I <u>never</u> feel part of the group.

A. Read the sight words above and the example sentence. Underline the sight words in 1—5 below.

1. My wife likes to go to every party, big or small.

2. I never want to go to a party where there are lots of people.

3. When I try to meet new people, I never know what to say.

4. I always feel better when I can bring my wife.

5. For a shy person like me, every party is lonely.

B. Choose the words below to finish the sentences.

party   every   bring   never

1. I _____ like big parties.

2. I feel like _____ other person here is having a good time.

3. There are a lot of good snacks at this _____.

4. When it's over, I hope we can _____ snacks home with us.

C. Read the sentences. Underline the sight words.

When I'm at a big party, I would like to feel better than I do. Every other person is having a good time, but I'm faking it. Being around people I don't know brings out my shyness. I never know the right thing to say. Does a big party make you feel this way?

Sight Words

belong   company   join   club

▶ I don't <u>join</u> the group at my wife's <u>company</u> party because I feel that I don't <u>belong</u>. It's like a <u>club</u>.

A. Read the sight words above and the example sentences. Underline the sight words in 1—5 below.

1. My wife's company gives a big party on a holiday.
2. She always asks me to join a group of her friends from work.
3. They talk about people and things from the company.
4. Because I don't know what they are talking about, I feel that I don't belong there.
5. I must learn how to join the club.

B. Choose the words below to finish the sentences.

belong   company   join   club

1. My wife works for a good _____.
2. All the workers feel that they _____.
3. It's much like joining a _____.
4. But when you don't work there, you can't always _____ the group.

C. Read the sentences. Underline the sight words.

When my wife's company gives a party, I don't have a good time. I feel like I'm on my own — that I don't belong to the group. I don't know how to join in the fun. Why do I feel that they have a club, and I don't belong to it?

Phonics: Silent Letters

A. **Listen to the sounds in each word. Underline each silent letter that stands for no sound.**

wr	kn	gu	gh
write	know	guitar	right
wrap	knit	guard	knight

B. **Make other words with *kn* or *wr*. Write each word and read it.**

kn + it   = _____   wr + it   = _____

kn + ock = _____   wr + ing = _____

kn + ot   = _____   wr + y   = _____

kn + ight = _____   wr + ap = _____

kn + ee   = _____   wr + en = _____

C. **Choose the correct word for each sentence below.**

1. (knock, know) I don't _____ what to say to people at a party.

2. (wring, writ) I stand at the back of the room and _____ my hands.

3. (knit, knee) I don't fit in with this tightly _____ group of people.

4. (wry, wrap) I hope they _____ up this party; I want to go home.

Phonics: -ing and -ub

bring

king

ring

sing

wing

A. Read the words in the box. Make other -ing words below.

spr + ing = _____

str + ing = _____

sw + ing = _____

wr + ing = _____

B. Read the sentences. Write an -ing word to finish each sentence.

1. Fran knows how to get into the _____ of things at a party.

2. She can _____ and play the guitar.

3. Fran likes to _____ friends to the party.

club

hub

rub

tub

A. Read the words in the box. Make other -ub words below.

gr + ub = _____

shr + ub = _____

sn + ub = _____

B. Read the sentences. Write an -ub word to finish each sentence.

1. How can I join this _____?

2. I feel that the people _____ me.

3. I must _____ people the wrong way.

Abbreviations and Titles

Doctor = Dr.   Company = Co.

An abbreviation is a short form of a word. Most abbreviations end with a period. An abbreviation that is part of a person's or place's name begins with a capital letter.

A. Read the words and write each abbreviation.

Missus = Mrs. _____   Street = St. _____

Mister = Mr. _____   Road = Rd. _____

Doctor = Dr. _____   Avenue = Ave. _____

ounce = oz. _____   pound = lb. _____

B. Practice reading the paragraph. Underline the abbreviations.

My wife works for the B. D. Clay Co. on Shell Ave. Mr. Clay is her boss. The company has a health plan with Dr. Peoples. The doctor works at Pope St. and School Rd. Mrs. Knight and I will see Dr. Peoples at the company party on Sunday, June 4.

C. Write the abbreviation for each name.

1. Doctor Key _____

2. Land Avenue _____

3. Missus Walker _____

4. Dean Company _____

5. Mister Hope _____

6. Dune Street _____

7. 5 ounces _____

8. Waters Road _____

Getting Over Shyness

Every time my wife's boss gives a company picnic or a party, I have a problem joining the group. Sometimes I feel that I don't belong with people I don't know. My wife knows that I hate going to these parties, but she always wants me to go with her. She is an out-going person, and she can't see why I have trouble talking to people.

I must get over this problem. Then I would not be lonely in a group of new people. I would have a good time and feel that I belong in the company club.

I'll talk with my friend Fran about my shyness. Fran sells homes to people in our city, and she is used to talking to people she does not know. Fran can make friends right away with no trouble. You might say that it's part of her job to be a good talker.

• • •

"To make friends, Rick, you have to be a friend. You don't have problems when you are around people you know, do you?" Fran asked.

"No, but then I know they like me," I said. "I keep thinking about that company party. Over and over I said the wrong things. I never want to go back to one again."

—Shyness—

"Tell me about it," said Fran. "Maybe I can give you some good tips that work for me."

"Sometimes I feel better when I have something to do with my hands. I carry a drink around with me, but at the other party, I spilled it all over the rug. When I try to think of the right thing to say, my mind is blank and the words don't come out right. See what I mean?" I asked.

"OK. Why don't we talk about some better ways to meet people at a party? When a person you don't know sits down by you, what do you say?" Fran asked.

"I try to give them a friendly greeting and tell them my name," I said.

"Is that all?"

"What do you want me to say?" I asked.

"Well, there are some things everyone wants to talk about. Ask about family, work, or school. Or a person may know a lot about something, like baseball or fine music. Another tip is to think about what you can give to the party. I know you can play the guitar well. Why not bring the guitar to the party and ask others to join in the singing? Or bring some games—people of all ages like games. When you are playing a game, you don't have time to think about what to say."

I need to think about Fran's tips. When I go to a party, it does not help to think about how shy I feel. I need to join in the fun, and I'll get my mind away from my own problems. Every party would be a chance to meet new people. After all, there might be other people in the group who feel shy, too. Maybe we could make our own club!

—Shyness—

After talking with Fran, I think I'm on the right road to overcoming my shyness. I'll never need to feel lonely in a group again.

Comprehension: Context

What Is Context?

Using context means learning a new word by looking at all the other words in a sentence or paragraph. When you use context, you decide what does and doesn't fit with the other words.

A. Read the tips and write your answers.

1. Read the sentence to the end; don't stop at the new word.

   Fran will **invite** all her friends to her party.

2. Think about what word makes sense.

   - Could it be *write*? _____ (*Clue*: That word would not make sense in the sentence.)

   - Could it be *ask*? _____ (That makes sense.)

B. The paragraph below has one word that you may not know. Use context to decide what the word means.

Rick has trouble talking to people he does not know. You could say he is a **bashful** person. He can't think of the right things to say. Maybe these people won't like him. Maybe they would like to spend time with other friends. The more Rick thinks about these things, the more shy he becomes.

A **bashful** person is _____.

bossy   shy   tired

Life Skill: Coping With Shyness

list   attention   relax

A. Read the new words above. Then read the tips below.

How To Cope With Shyness

1. Look right at a friendly face when you are talking before a group. Think about the worst mistake you could make and laugh about it. Ask "If I flub a line in my talk, will everyone get up and walk out? No!"

2. Don't make up for shyness by being bossy. You may not want others to know how you feel, but being bossy isn't good.

3. Get other people to talk. Then stop thinking about you and pay attention to what they are saying.

4. Don't make up for shyness by drinking too much. You may think it will help you talk, but you'll say the wrong thing.

5. Relax! There will be other shy people around. You are more like other people than you are different.

B. Read the questions and write the answers.

1. Most of the list tells you what to do about shyness. Which sentences tells you what <u>not</u> to do?

   _____

   _____

2. Which three things in the list might be the most helpful to you? Why?

   _____

   _____

   _____

3. Tip #5 says, "You are more like other people than you are different." What does this sentence mean?

   _____

   _____

A Singer's Life

Jill sat still and let the music carry her back in time. In her mind, she was a singer again—a big name with a swing band at the Black Hat Club. When she was singing at the club, people would stand in line a long time for a good seat. The fans loved her, and she got a lot of attention from them.

Her boss said she could go a long way as a singer. It would take time, work, and luck, but she could be a big star. "Stick to it, Jill," he had said. "You and the band will make it. You are a winning team. One of these days, you will cut a hit record that will take you right to the top!"

That had been a different time in Jill's life. What grand plans she had had! But life does not always go the way you want it to go.

Jill got up and greeted the woman who walked into the Women's Room. The woman ran some cold water in the sink, and Jill helped her dry her hands. Before she went back to her table, the woman dropped some money in Jill's hand.

Jill took her seat again. She might as well relax. It would be a long night.

Review Words

A. Check the words you know.

- ☐ 1. been
- ☐ 2. cold
- ☐ 3. record
- ☐ 4. mind
- ☐ 5. seat
- ☐ 6. right
- ☐ 7. star
- ☐ 8. team
- ☐ 9. women
- ☐ 10. took
- ☐ 11. what
- ☐ 12. when

B. Read and write these sentences.

1. What a chance I took when I joined a group of women singers!

_____

_____

2. It's been a lot of work, but I don't mind.

_____

3. We've become big stars, and people spend a lot of money for seats to see us.

_____

_____

C. Match each word and its meaning.

_____ 1. cold   a. not wrong

_____ 2. record   b. not hot

_____ 3. right   c. group of players

_____ 4. team   d. recorded music

Sight Words

once   attendant   now   career

▶ Jill is an <u>attendant</u> <u>now</u>, but <u>once</u> she had a <u>career</u> as a singer.

A. Read the sight words above and the example sentence. Underline the sight words in 1—5 below.

1. Once Jill hoped for a career in music.
2. She planned her life around a career as a singer.
3. Jill gave up her plans once she had a family.
4. Now Jill has a different career at a nightclub.
5. She works as an attendant in the Women's Room.

B. Choose the words below to finish the sentences.

Now   Once   career   attendant

1. It takes a long time to make a _____ in music.

2. _____ Jill had the time to be a singer.

3. _____ that Jill has a family, things are different.

4. Jill took a job as an _____ because she needed the money.

C. Read the sentences. Underline the sight words.

Jill quit school to work on her career as a singer. She did not learn to read or write well. When her singing career did not work out, Jill needed to find a job. Now she is an attendant in a nightclub. Being an attendant isn't the career she once wanted, but she still has hopes for a different life.

Sight Words

listen   **your**   **sweep**   **if**

▶ If your job is in a nightclub, you can listen to music when you sweep.

A. **Read the sight words above and the example sentence. Underline the sight words in 1—4 below.**

1. Jill likes to listen to the music at the club.
2. When she gets to the club, she sweeps the Women's Room.
3. If she has time, she listens to Bing play old tunes.
4. She says, "Your music sweeps me back in time."

B. **Choose the words below to finish the sentences.**

If   listen   sweep   your

1. It's not fun to _____ up, but it's a job.
2. _____ you do a job well, you feel good.
3. You must do what is right for _____ life at the time.
4. Jill must _____ to the needs of her family.

C. **Read the sentences. Underline the sight words.**

If you work at night, your bedtime is different from other people's. When Jill comes home, she gets the children up. She may be tired, but she has to sweep up at home, too. Then she cooks some food and listens as the kids plan a new school day.

Jill wants her kids to have a different life from her own. "Things will be better if you stay in school and learn all the skills you can," she tells them. "Listen to the words of one who knows."

Sight Words

89

customer   year   blues   piano

▶ For years, customers have listened to Bing play the blues at the piano.

A. Read the sight words above and the example sentence. Underline the sight words in 1—4 below.

1. Jill and Bing have been friends for years.
2. Bing is one of the best piano players in the city.
3. Customers flock to the club to listen to him.
4. Bing plays some old blues songs for Jill.

B. Choose the words below to finish the sentences.

blues   years   customers   piano

1. "This club could use a good _____ singer," Bing told the boss.
2. He should know; Bing has been playing the _____ for years.
3. Mr. Drake did not think his _____ would like a blues singer.
4. Some _____ back the club had a singer, but it did not pay.

C. Read the sentences. Underline the sight words.

A club owner will always try to give the customers what they want. They come to listen to Bing play blues music on the piano.

"This club has been doing well for years," Mr. Drake told Bing. "After all these years, why should I do things differently? Jill is a good attendant, but I don't know if she can sing the blues, and I don't think the customers will go for something different."

Phonics: Y as a Vowel

why   baby

y = long i   y = long e

A. Read the words and listen for the last vowel sound. Write the word and circle the letter that stands for the last sound.

1. why _____   1. lucky _____

2. my _____   2. carry _____

3. by _____   3. party _____

4. dry _____   4. lonely _____

B. Read the words. Then write each word under the right heading.

sly
try
baby
healthy
cry
many
heavy
fly

y = long i	y = long e
1. _____	1. _____
2. _____	2. _____
3. _____	3. _____
4. _____	4. _____

C. Read the sentences. Circle the y words with the long *i* sound. Underline the y words with the long e sound.

1. Jill can carry a tune well.

2. She wants to try to sing at the party.

3. Many people want her to try.

4. Jill is lucky that people try to get her to sing.

Phonics: -*eep* and -*ear*

sweep
deep
jeep
keep

A. Read the words in the box. Make other -*eep* words below.

sh + eep = _____

sl + eep = _____

st + eep = _____

B. Read the sentences. Write an -*eep* word to finish each sentence.

1. Because she works at night, Jill must _____ in the daytime.

2. She must _____ her job as an attendant to bring in money for her family.

3. But, down _____, Jill longs to be a big star as a blues singer.

year
dear
fear
hear
near

A. Read the words in the box. Make other -*ear* words below.

cl + ear = _____

sh + ear = _____

sm + ear = _____

B. Read the sentences. Write an -*ear* word to finish each sentence.

1. Bing is a _____ friend of Jill's.

2. "If you want to _____ a good singer," he told Mr. Drake, "listen to Jill."

3. "She will do a good job once she gets over her _____."

Days and Months

January = Jan. Sunday = Sun.

The name of each day of the week and month of the year begins with a capital letter. You can write the days and most of the months in a short form. These abbreviations begin with a capital letter and end with a period.

A. Read each word and its abbreviation. Write the abbreviations.

Sunday   = Sun. _____   Thursday = Thurs. _____

Monday   = Mon. _____   Friday   = Fri.   _____

Tuesday = Tues. _____   Saturday = Sat.   _____

Wednesday = Wed. _____

B. Read each word and its abbreviation. Write the short forms.

January   = Jan. _____   August   = Aug. _____

February = Feb. _____   September = Sept. _____

March   = Mar. _____   October   = Oct. _____

April   = Apr. _____   November = Nov. _____

May, June, July   December = Dec. _____

C. Practice reading the paragraphs. Underline the names of months and days.

On Sunday and Monday, no one comes to the Black Hat Club. On Tuesday, Wednesday, and Thursday, some people drop by after work. Most of our customers come in on Friday and Saturday.

The club always has lots of customers in December, because it's a holiday time. It's cold in January and February, and people don't get out much. In the spring, people drop in again.

Singing the Blues

It had been a long day at home, and now Jill had her night job at the club to do. She was on her way to the Women's Room when Bing called to her. "Jill, sit with me before you go to work. I want to talk to you about something."

Jill went over to the piano and took a seat by Bing. "The boss and I have been talking about getting a singer in the club," Bing said. "He thinks we don't need one, but you know I feel differently. For a long time I've been saying that the nights in here would be better if I had a singer working with me. I want that singer to be you."

Jill looked blank. "What do you mean, me? I was a blues singer once, but I haven't worked at that career in years. I never made a go of it. Now, being an attendant isn't a lot of fun, but I do make money at it, and I keep my job."

Bing said, "Listen, Jill, I know all about that. But I want you to try the blues once more. Come on, the boss won't mind."

Jill laughed and said, "OK, I'll try it once. Then I'll get on with my sweeping."

"I'll pick one of your big hits," Bing said. "How about 'Lonely Woman'?" Once the music got going, Jill did not take long to get with the beat. It was like the music belonged to Jill, and she belonged to it.

—Blues—

They did not know it, but the boss had been sitting at the back of the club. Mr. Drake and two good customers were at a small table at the end of the room. When Jill stopped, the customers yelled, "Once more, Jill! Sing again!"

Jill laughed. She was feeling bashful because she did not know customers were in the club. But she could not stop now! Bing was playing 'Country Blues', and the music took her away again. Soon, the customers and the boss came over to the piano.

"What are you doing sweeping up a women's room?" Mr. Drake asked. "I did not know you could sing like that, Jill! From now on, I want you to stop all that cleaning and work with Bing every night. The two of you make an outstanding team. How about it?"

—Blues—

Jill looked at Bing and laughed. Then she looked at her boss. "Listen, Mr. Drake," she said, "singing for customers is what I like best of all. I took a shot at it once when I was a kid. I cut two records, but they never sold well. I know I was good, and I had hopes of being a big star. But a singing career can be a bad life. I have a family now, and I need a daily income. Right now, as an attendant, I have that."

"I know what you mean, Jill," Mr. Drake said. "But I'll pay you every night, if you sing or sweep the Women's Room. And if you sing like you did here, your tips will bring in lots more money."

"Will you give it a chance, Jill?" asked Bing. "The boss can get someone to clean for you. The years go by, and you don't always get a shot at a new career."

"Bing, you are a dear friend, and I thank you for your help," Jill said. "But I do have a lot of fears— about a new career and my family's needs. Mr. Drake, will my attendant's job still be there if I don't make it singing in your club?"

"You bet!" said Mr. Drake. "But I think you'll never want to go back to your old job again!"

"Well, I never hoped to get another chance at this late date," said Jill, "but you are right, Bing. I can't let this chance go by. I'm willing to give a singer's life one more try."

Comprehension: Context

What Is Context?

Using context means learning a new word by looking at all the other words in a sentence or paragraph. When you use context, you decide what does and doesn't fit with the other words.

A. Read the tips and write your answers.

1. Read the sentence to the end.

   Jill did not **enjoy** her job in the Women's Room.

2. Think about what word makes sense.

   - Could it be *need*? _____ (*Clue*: You know that Jill needs her job.)

   - Could it be *do*? _____ (*Clue:* You know that Jill does her job well.)

   - Could it be *like*? _____ (That makes sense.)

B. The paragraph below has a word that you may not know. Use context to decide what the word means.

When Jill hears an old blues tune, she thinks about the old days. "I **remember** how it used to be over at the Black Hat," she tells Bing. "I think back about how fearful I was at first, and I **remember** all the people who came to hear me sing."

To remember means to:

a. talk something over with a friend.
b. think back about something or someone.
c. feel fearful about something.

Life Skill: Reading a Schedule

event   schedule   longest

A. Read the new words above. Then read the schedule of events below.

COME AND GET IT DAYS

Haystack Park
Lake City, Ohio

SCHEDULE OF EVENTS

Thursday, June 16, 1988

7:30 P.M.	Haystack Park Parade
	Lake City's School Marching Bands

Friday, June 17, 1988

12:00 noon – 2:00 P.M.	Children's Play "Jack & the Beanstalk"
2:00 P.M. – 6:00 P.M.	Old Movies: "Woman of the Year",
	"To Have and Have Not"
2:00 P.M. – 3:00 P.M.	The Dean Brothers (piano group)
5:00 P.M. – 7:30 P.M.	Family Cook-Out in the park
8:00 P.M. – 12:00 A.M.	"Come and Get It Days" Sock Hop

Saturday, June 18, 1988

10:00 A.M. – 11:00 A.M.	The New Tunes (swing band)
1:00 P.M. – 5:30 P.M.	Old Movies: "The Thin Man",
	"Some Like It Hot"
1:00 P.M. – 5:30 P.M.	Games for the family
5:30 P.M. – 8:00 P.M.	Lake City Food Bank Dinner
	down-home cooking, $7.50 plate

—Tickets will be sold to customers at the gate—

B. Read the questions and write the answers.

1. If your job ends at 4:00 P.M. on Friday, which event could you go to right after work?

_____

2. On which day do the events go on for the longest time?

_____

_____

UNIT 1 Review

A. Write the words below in the sentences.

roommate	save	how	spend
coupons	then	why	think
could	cost	too	much

1. Cutting out _____ can take a lot of time.

2. _____ they help us save on something we need?

3. My _____ says that coupons can help us save money.

4. Do you _____ my roommate is right about coupons?

B. Write -ink or -y to make new words. Then write each word in a sentence.

1. wh + _ = _____   _____ did I buy all this pop?

2. dr + ___ = _____   I can't _____ all of it.

3. tr + _ = _____   I'll _____ to take it back.

4. th + ___ = _____   Do you _____ the store will take it back?

C. Complete the sentence by choosing the verb that tells about the past.

1. Someone at the store _____ my roommate a new radio.

sell   sold

2. The trouble was that Kay _____ too much for it.

paid   pay

3. It _____ me mad to find out that my sister _____ a lot of money.

make   made   spent   spend

UNIT 2 Review

A. Write the words below in the sentences.

always	meet	or	after
school	soon	means	where
report	must	card	grades

1. Mr. Sanders _____ wanted to learn to read well.

2. He wants Jay to get good _____ in reading.

3. That _____ Jay will have to do all his homework.

4. Jay _____ come home right _____ school.

B. Write -eet or -ean to make new words. Then write each word in a sentence.

1. m + ____ = _____   Mr. Sanders will _____ Jay's teacher.

2. gr + ____ = _____   She will _____ him with a handshake.

3. J + ____ = _____   Jay's teacher is Mrs. _____ Keating.

4. m + ____ = _____   She isn't a _____ teacher.

C. Write the correct word in the sentences.

1. A person who can't read is _____ for some jobs.

unfit
unlucky

_____

2. Jay must _____ things many times.

rerun
reread

_____

3. I'll _____ Jay to do his homework.

repay
remind

_____

4. Jay thinks he is _____ to have a mean teacher.

unlucky
unsold

_____

UNIT 3 Review

A. Write the words below in the sentences.

know	tired	late	before
rock	small	new	pregnant
wife	baby	as	responsible

1. My _____ and I will soon be parents.

2. We're both _____ for looking after the baby.

3. _____ the baby comes, I'll need to learn many things.

4. Is there a school for _____ parents?

B. Write -ate or -ock to make new words. Then write each word in a sentence.

1. pl + ____ = _____   A new baby can't eat from a _____.

2. bl + ____ = _____   Babies like to play with this _____.

3. l + ____ = _____   Will Carlos have to get up _____ at night?

4. r + ____ = _____   He may have to _____ the baby.

C. Add -ies to the words. Write the correct words in the sentences below.

baby _____   family _____

cry _____   country _____

1. We know that our _____ will be glad about the baby.

2. We won't mind when the baby's _____ wake us.

3. Someday we want to have more _____.

4. Many _____ have laws that help children.

UNIT 4 Review

A. Write the words below in the sentences.

around	park	thank	foreign
summer	cook	grass	snacks
picnic	jump	rules	saw

1. On a summer day, many people go to the _____.

2. First they should stop and read the park _____.

3. Then they can run _____ and play games.

4. When they get hot, they can _____ in the lake and swim.

B. Write -*ack* or -*ank* to make new words. Then write each word in a sentence.

1. p + ___ = _____   The Baker family will _____ a big picnic bag.

2. b + ___ = _____   They'll go _____ to the old tables by the lake.

3. bl + ___ = _____   They saw lots of _____ bugs by the food.

4. b + ___ = _____   Mrs. Baker likes to sit on the _____.

C. Write the correct word in the sentences.

1. We have a _____ of people to take to the park.   playful
                                                            carful

_____

2. Thank _____ Dad has a big van.   goodness
                                            sickness

_____

3. I'm lucky to have _____ children.   helpful
                                               carful

_____

UNIT 5 Review

A. Write the words below in the sentences.

here	put	pick	lesson
long	kid	again	straight
away	been	still	sentence

1. Sly has ——————— in prison much of his life.

2. He found out that a prison ——————— is a ticket to nowhere.

3. Sly has spent a ——————— time in a prison cell.

4. He may have learned his ——————— too late in life.

B. Write *-ick* or *-ill* to make new words. Then write each word in a sentence.

1. qu + ——— = ———————   There is no ——————— way to do time.

2. p + ——— = ———————   Sometimes the guards ——————— on you.

3. f + ——— = ———————   You try to find some way to ——————— the time.

4. st + ——— = ———————   But the days are ——————— too long.

C. Write the correct word in the sentences.

1. Some of Chet's friends are ——————— to get him in trouble. differently likely

2. Chet thinks shoplifting is a ——————— way to get what he wants. handy bossy

3. I can see he is making some ——————— mistakes. fatherly costly

UNIT 6 Review

A. Write the words below in the sentences.

club	every	ask	better
join	party	would	belong
over	bring	never	company

1. I —————— can relax at big parties.

2. I ————— like to have a good time in a group of new people.

3. Somehow I feel like I don't —————.

4. ————— time I try to say something, the words come out wrong.

B. Write _-ub_ or _-ing_ to make new words. Then write each word in a sentence.

1. cl + ＿＿ = —————   Why did I join this —————?

2. sn + ＿＿ = —————   Maybe the people here will not ————— me.

3. sw + ＿＿＿ = —————   I need to learn how to get in the ————— of things.

4. br + ＿＿＿ = —————   Maybe it would help to ————— some of my own friends.

C. Draw lines to match the words and abbreviations.

1. Street   oz.

2. pound   Dr.

3. Avenue   St.

4. Missus   Ave.

5. ounces   Mrs.

6. Doctor   lb.

UNIT 7 Review

A. Write the words below in the sentences.

once	if	sweep	listen
blue	now	piano	customer
year	your	career	attendant

1. _____ Jill was a blues singer at the Black Hat.

2. When her _____ did not work out, she needed another job.

3. _____ she is an attendant at a nightclub.

4. It's not fun to _____ up, but it brings in money.

B. Write -ear or -eep to make new words. Then write each word in a sentence.

1. y + ___ = _____   Bing has been playing the piano for more

  than a _____ .

2. f + ___ = _____   He knows Jill needs time to get over her

  _____ .

3. d + ___ = _____   Down _____ , Jill longs to be a singer.

4. k + ___ = _____   She must _____ her job.

C. Draw lines to match the words and abbreviations.

1. Wednesday   Dec.

2. February   Apr.

3. Tuesday   Thurs.

4. December   Wed.

5. Thursday   Tues.

6. April   Feb.

Word List

Below is a list of the 355 words that are presented to students in *Book 4* of *Reading for Today*. These words will be reviewed in later books. The numeral following each word refers to the page on which the word is introduced to students.

A

after	18
again	61
always	17
Apr.	92
April	92
around	45
as	31
ask	73
attendant	87
attention	83
Aug.	92
August	92
Ave.	78
away	60

B

babies	36
baby	31
back	49
badly	64
bank	49
bashful	82
bean	21
been	59
beet	21
before	32
belong	75
best	27
better	73
black	49
blank	49
blend	34
blight	34
blink	34
block	35
blue	89
bossy	64
boldness	50
bought	8
brag	6
brand	6
bring	74
brink	7

C

card	19
career	87
carful	50
chill	63
chin	48
cities	36
clan	34
clean	21
clear	91
clink	34
clock	35
club	75
company	75
cook	46
cost	4
costly	64
could	3
countries	36
coupon	3
cream	6
cries	36
crop	6
cry	7
customer	89

D

daily	41
date	35
Dean	21
dear	91
Dec.	92
December	92
deep	91
differently	64
Dr.	78
drank	49
drink	7
drip	6
drug	6
dry	7

E

enjoy	96
event	97
every	74